Milton Hershey's Sweet Idea

A Chocolate Kingdom

by Sharon Katz Cooper   illustrated by Alvaro Iglesias Sánchez

PICTURE WINDOW BOOKS
a capstone imprint

Milton Hershey's father was a dreamer who did poorly in business. He struggled to provide for his family. But he always believed something good was going to happen. He passed that belief on to his son. It helped Milton get through many bad times in his life.

Milton Hershey was born on a Pennsylvania farm in 1857. At age 14 he started work at a candy shop in Lancaster. He studied with the candy-maker and learned quickly. He dreamed of becoming a great candy-maker someday.

When Milton's apprenticeship ended in 1876, his mother gave him some advice. "Milton," she said, "you are now going out into the world to make a man of yourself. My best advice to you is this: When you tackle a job, stick to it until you have mastered it."

Milton borrowed $150 from his aunt and went to Philadelphia. There, at age 18, he opened his first shop. His mother and aunt helped him make candy every night. But the shop did not make enough money. After six years Milton closed it.

Next, Milton moved to Denver, Colorado. He got a job with another candy-maker. He learned a new way of making caramels. Fresh milk was the key!

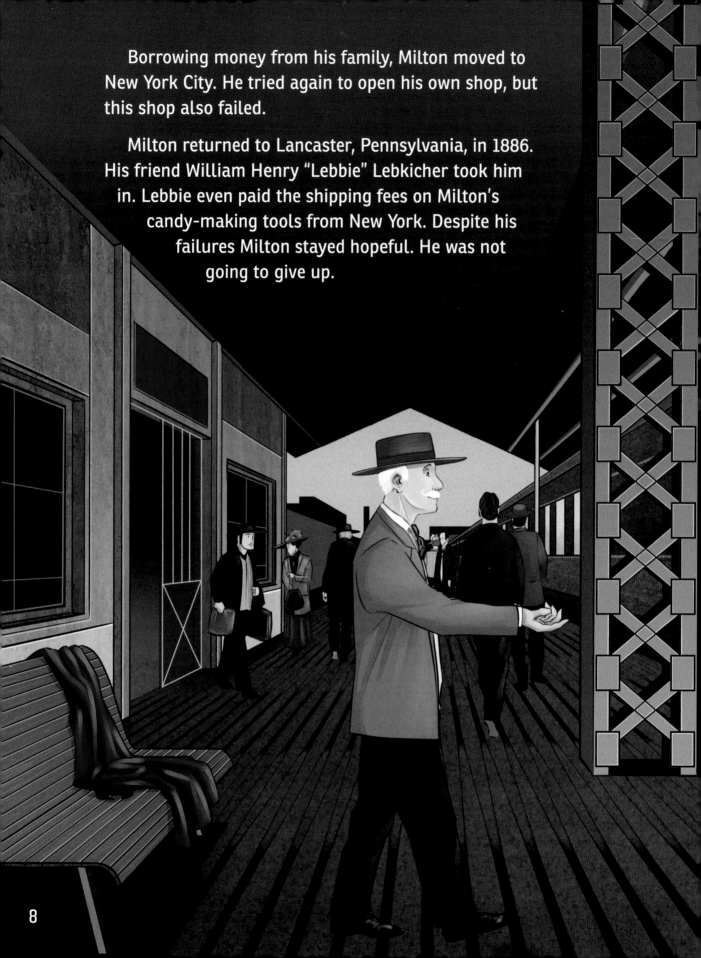

Borrowing money from his family, Milton moved to New York City. He tried again to open his own shop, but this shop also failed.

Milton returned to Lancaster, Pennsylvania, in 1886. His friend William Henry "Lebbie" Lebkicher took him in. Lebbie even paid the shipping fees on Milton's candy-making tools from New York. Despite his failures Milton stayed hopeful. He was not going to give up.

Milton asked his aunt, Mattie, for financial help. He wanted to use the skills he'd learned in Denver to make caramels. Aunt Mattie agreed, and Milton started the Lancaster Caramel Company. He worked tirelessly. Every day he walked several miles to a dairy farm to pick up fresh milk for his caramels.

A short time later, a man from England stopped by Milton's shop. He tasted the caramels, loved them, and placed a huge order. He promised to pay when the candies arrived in London. "If this works," he said, "I will order much more."

Milton went to the bank. He explained about the Englishman's order and the need for machines and supplies to fill the order. With Aunt Mattie's help, Milton got a 90-day loan.

Near the end of his 90 days, Milton grew nervous. He couldn't pay back the money. Plus, he wanted to borrow another $1,000 to buy more equipment and supplies. He went back to the bank and told the bank manager, Frank Brenneman, that he needed more time and money. Frank saw something promising in the struggling candy-maker. But Milton was a big risk for the bank to take. "I don't know," Frank said. "Come back tomorrow."

Milton went home and hoped for something good to happen. And it did.

The next day Milton got his extra time and money.
Frank put the loan in his own name and then lent the
money to Milton. Milton worked day and night. He filled
the large order and shipped it off.

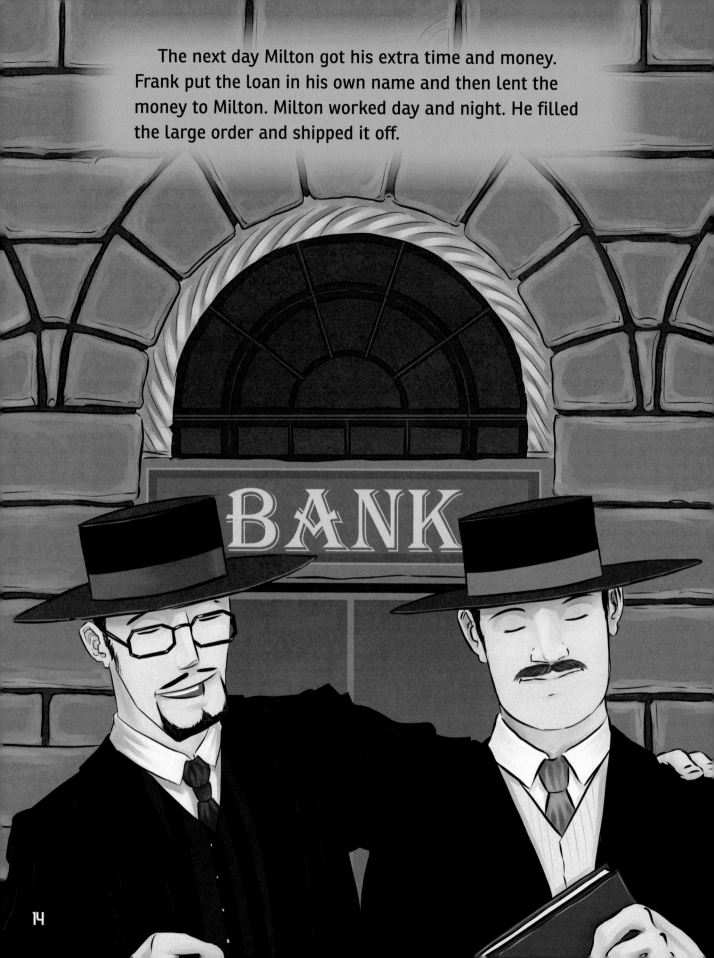

With only a few days left on his loan, a check arrived in the mail from London. Milton was able to pay off his debt. Other orders rolled in. By the 1890s, caramels had made Milton Hershey a millionaire.

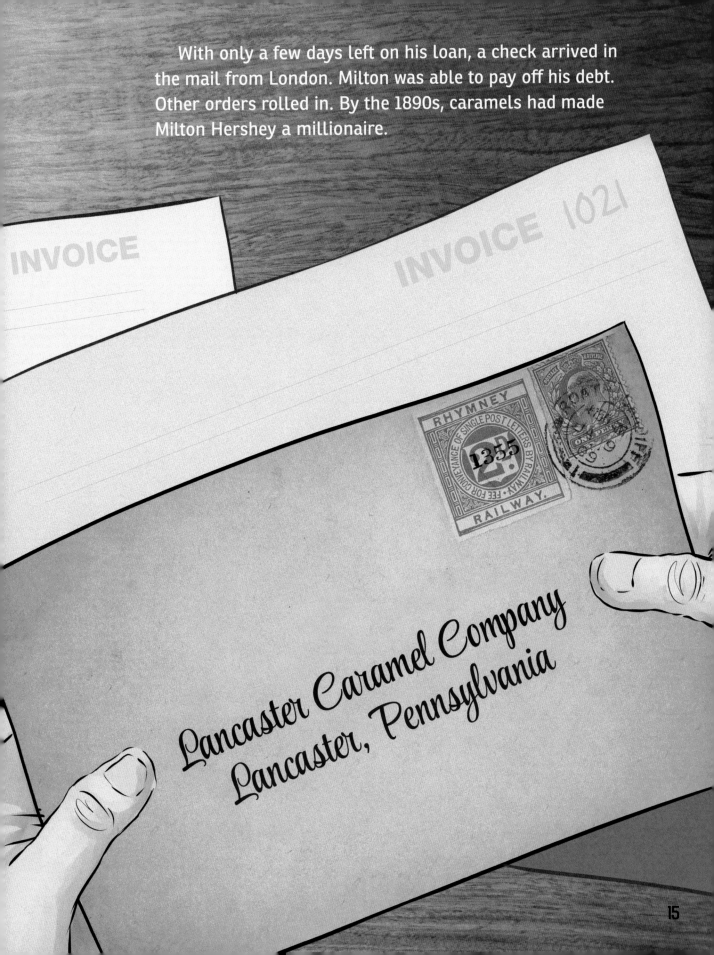

INVOICE

INVOICE 1021

RHYMNEY
FEE FOR CONVEYANCE OF SINGLE POST LETTERS BY RAILWAY.
2D.
1355
RAILWAY.

Lancaster Caramel Company
Lancaster, Pennsylvania

Chicago, Illinois, hosted the World's Fair in 1893. Milton went and saw a display of chocolate-making machines from Germany. He watched the machines work. He smelled and tasted the chocolate. He told the owner he wanted to buy the equipment.

As soon as the fair ended, the German shipped two machines to the Lancaster Caramel Company. "Caramels are a fad," Milton said, "but chocolate is permanent. I am going to make chocolate."

In the 1890s no one in the United States made milk chocolate candy. It was a luxury imported from Switzerland and sold in fancy stores. Most Americans could not afford it. Milton wanted to create milk chocolate that everyone—rich or poor—could enjoy.

Milton had done well with caramels
by adding fresh milk. He wanted to
do the same with chocolate. He had
no background in chemistry or food
science. He simply tried and tried
again—for months. He worked behind
closed doors. Sometimes he did not
even stop for meals.

Eventually Milton came up with a way (still a secret) to make his perfect milk chocolate. He sold the caramel company in 1900 for $1 million. He bought a large piece of land in Derry Township, Pennsylvania, near his childhood home. On this land, in 1903, he started building his giant chocolate factory.

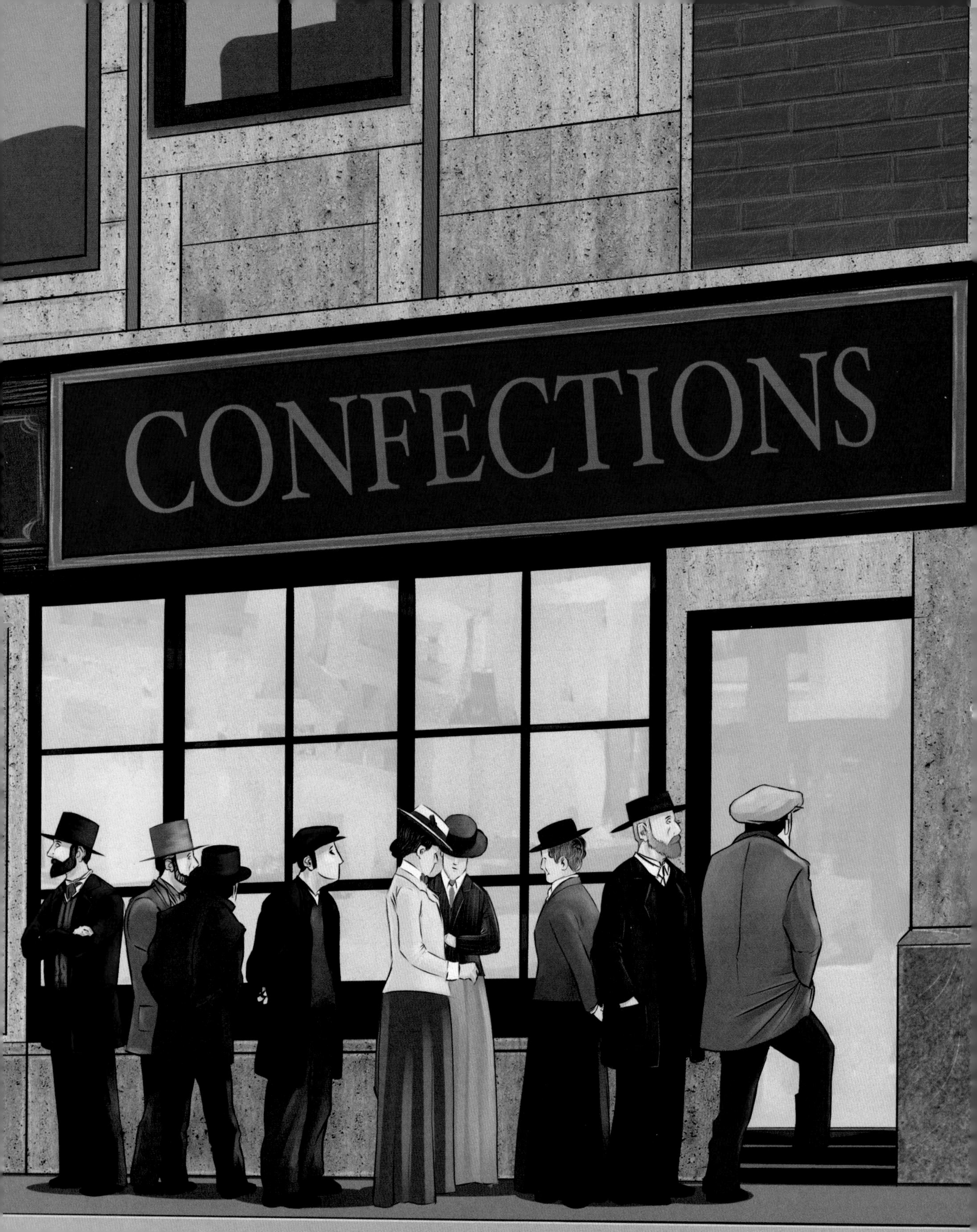
CONFECTIONS

The Hershey's Milk Chocolate bar we know today appeared in 1900. It cost little and tasted good. Milton worked hard to keep production costs as low as possible. It was important to him that everyone could buy his chocolate. The first Hershey's Milk Chocolate bars cost five cents each.

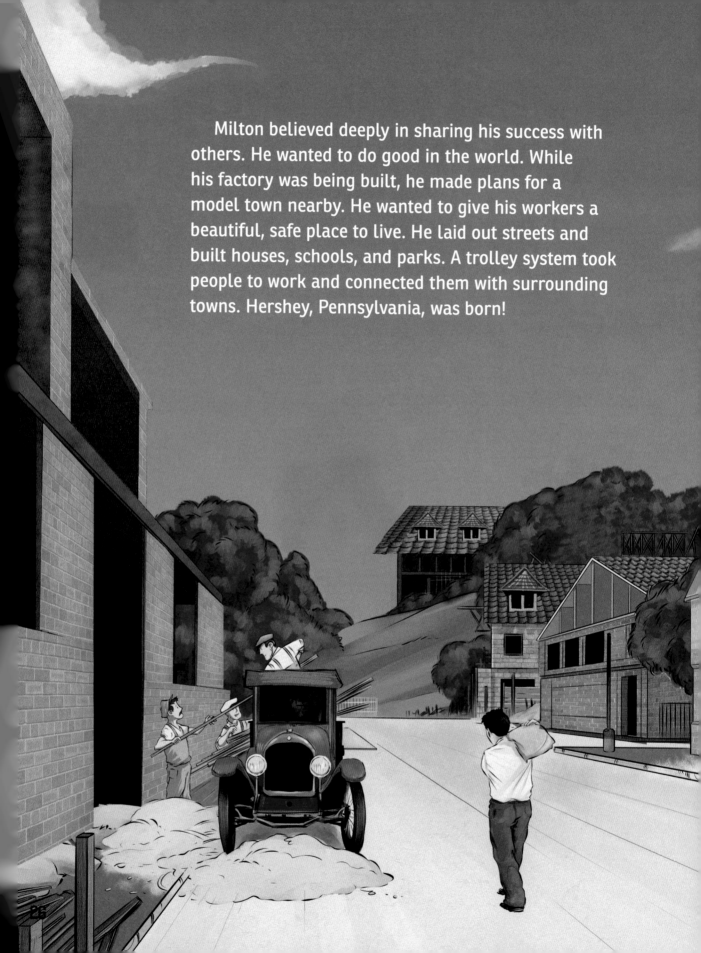

Milton believed deeply in sharing his success with others. He wanted to do good in the world. While his factory was being built, he made plans for a model town nearby. He wanted to give his workers a beautiful, safe place to live. He laid out streets and built houses, schools, and parks. A trolley system took people to work and connected them with surrounding towns. Hershey, Pennsylvania, was born!

Milton never stopped dreaming and doing. Production improved. New products were made. The town of Hershey kept growing.

Milton believed in hard work, generosity, and honesty. "Whatever money you ... earn during your lifetime," he said, "use it wisely. Spend it for the good of others, and you will be richly rewarded."

Milton and his wife, Kitty, were unable to have children of their own. Instead, they used part of their fortune to open a school for orphaned boys. The school opened in September 1910 with four students. After Kitty died at age 42, Milton donated all of his money to the school—more than $60 million! Today, the school is called the Milton Hershey School. More than 2,000 students—boys and girls—attend each year.

Milton Hershey died in 1945, at age 88. Today, The Hershey Company employs more than 13,000 people around the world.

Milton Hershey, circa 1924

Hersheypark, Hershey, Pennsylvania

Glossary

apprenticeship—a work arrangement in which someone works for a skilled person, often for a basic wage, in order to learn that person's skills

chemistry—the scientific study of substances, what they are made of, and the ways they react with each other

debt—money that a person owes

fad—something that is very popular for a short period of time

financial—having to do with money

generosity—a willingness to give to others

import—to bring goods into one country from another

loan—money that is borrowed with a plan to pay it back

luxury—something that is not needed but adds great ease and comfort

orphaned—to have both parents die

permanent—lasting for a long time or forever

production—the making of something

risk—a chance of loss or harm

trolley—an electric streetcar that runs on tracks and gets power from an overhead wire

Critical Thinking Using the Common Core

1. Name the problems Milton ran into while trying to build his chocolate kingdom. Then describe how he solved each of them. **[Key Ideas and Details]**

2. Before he left home, Milton's mother gave him this advice: "When you tackle a job, stick to it until you have mastered it." Explain how Milton followed this advice. **[Craft and Structure]**

3. Describe the roles Aunt Mattie, Frank Brenneman, and the Englishman played in the success of Milton's caramel company in Lancaster. **[Key Ideas and Details]**

Read More

Buckley, James, Jr. *Who Was Milton Hershey?* Who Was ...? New York: Grosset & Dunlap, 2013.

Mattern, Joanne. *Milton Hershey: Hershey's Chocolate Creator.* Food Dudes. Minneapolis: Abdo Pub.: 2015.

Polin, C. J. *The Story of Chocolate.* DK Readers. 3, Reading Alone. New York: DK Pub., 2005.

Internet Sites

FactHound offers a safe, fun way to find Internet sites related to this book. All of the sites on FactHound have been researched by our staff.

Here's all you do:

Visit *www.facthound.com*

Type in this code: 9781479571376

 **Super-cool stuff!** Check out projects, games and lots more at www.capstonekids.com

Look for all the books in the series:

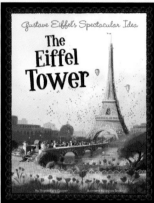

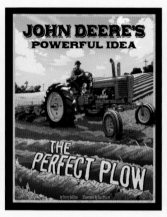

Special thanks to our advisers for their expertise:
Pamela Whitenack, Director, Hershey Community Archives
Hershey, Pennsylvania

Terry Flaherty, PhD, Professor of English
Minnesota State University, Mankato

Editor: Jill Kalz
Designer: Lori Bye
Creative Director: Nathan Gassman
Production Specialist: Laura Manthe
The illustrations in this book were created digitally.

Picture Window Books are published by Capstone,
1710 Roe Crest Drive, North Mankato, Minnesota 56003
www.capstonepub.com

Corbis/Bettmann, 29 (right), Shutterstock/Lissandra Melo, 29
(top and bottom left)

Library of Congress Cataloging-in-Publication Data
Katz Cooper, Sharon.
  Milton Hershey's sweet idea : a chocolate kingdom / by Sharon
Katz Cooper.
      pages cm.—(Picture Window Books. The story behind the name)
  Includes bibliographical references and index.
  Audience: K to Grade 3.
  Summary: "Discusses the invention of the Hershey bar and the man
behind it, including the idea, the obstacles, and the eventual success"—
Provided by publisher.
  ISBN 978-1-5158-1261-6 (hardcover)
1. Hershey Foods Corporation—History—Juvenile literature.
2. Businesspeople—United States—Biography—Juvenile literature.
3. Chocolate industry—United States—History—Juvenile literature.
4. Hershey, Milton Snavely, 1857–1945. I. Title.
  HD9200.U52K38 2015
  338.7'664153092—dc23
  [B]   2014049211

Printed in China.
007804